Word Games

By the same authors
More Word Games

Published by arrangement with the British Broadcasting Corporation

Word Games

Sandy Brownjohn and Janet Whitaker

Illustrated by Toni Goffe

HODDER AND STOUGHTON
LONDON SYDNEY AUCKLAND TORONTO

ISBN 0 340 38132 9 (Bds)
ISBN 0 340 36012 7 (Pbk)

First published 1985

Printed and bound in Hong Kong for
Hodder and Stoughton Educational,
a division of Hodder and Stoughton Ltd,
Mill Road, Dunton Green, Sevenoaks, Kent,
by Colorcraft Ltd
Photoset in Univers Medium by
Rowland Phototypesetting Ltd,
Bury St Edmunds, Suffolk

Contents

Introduction

Word Games started life as a series of BBC School Radio programmes. Sandy wrote them and Janet produced them. For those of you who enjoy playing games, in this book you will find a bran tub into which you can dip at will.

You will find party games, jokes, invented words, puns, rhymes and wordplay of all kinds that you can try out with your friends. There are poems and songs, too, which we chose because we liked the way the poets had enjoyed using the language.

There is no need to read this book from front to back, or even from back to front, just open it anywhere and enjoy playing with words. See what you can do with them. You'll be surprised.

We should like to thank all those who have helped *Word Games* on its way. Particular thanks go to Denise Coffey, Vicky Ireland and Ken Shanley, the actors, who made the scripts come alive and, we hope, had fun in the process. Thanks also are due to Janet Maybin, Marion Conry and Yvonne Klemperer for the work they put in on the programmes and the books. Last, but definitely not least, a special thanks to Diana Simons, possibly the best editor in the business!

Sandy Brownjohn and *Janet Whitaker*

AS EASY AS A B C

Roll up, Roll up, Ladies and Gentlemen.
This way to the Alphabet Fantasy Funfair.
Step forward. Don't be shy. Take a ride on
the ghastly ghost train. Scream your way
through the haunted ABC. From Apparition
to Zombie – a catalogue of catastrophe,
an alphabetical ride you'll never forget.

A for an apparition that appears without arms,
B for a black bat that blunders and alarms.
C for a cockroach that creeps into your brain,
D for Dracula drinking blood from a vein.
E for an eerie echo extended in the mind,
F for a face that floats in front and behind.
G for the ghost that glides all ghastly white,
H for the cry of HELP! in a hopeless fright.
I for the icy invisible hand of fear,
J for the jitters and the jangling chains you hear.
K for the kookaburra laughing fit to kill,
L for the lopsided leer that gives a thrill.
M for midnight when magic is abroad,
N for nightmares and the nervous tightening cord.
O for the owl, silent ghost of the dark,
P for the phantom whose footprints leave no mark.
Q for the quagmire that quivers and quakes,
R for repulsive rats and rattlesnakes.
S for the spectre that screams and sighs,
T for the tarantula that terrifies.
U for the unearthly UFO,
V for the vampire who vanishes below.
W for the werewolf who wails at the moon,
X for the X-ray of a skeleton's bones.
Y for a yell and a yawning moan,
Z for a zombie from the twilight zone.

Did You Know?

You are using NOUNS all the time. Everything that has a name is a NOUN – funfair, ghost, train, werewolf, zombie, vampire, are all NOUNS.

Word Game

Nouns are magic – give something a name and you conjure up a picture of it. Can you write your own ABC? Instead of a Ghost Train, you might try a Ship's ABC, Animals, Food, or anything else you like.

You, yourself, are a NOUN – boy or girl, brother or sister, daughter or son. And you are also a PROPER NOUN when you use your name, e.g. Neil, Joan, Barbara, Michael.

HALL OF MIRRORS

Mirror, mirror on the wall,
Who is the fairest of them all?

See yourself as others see you!
Pause a while for reflection.

Mirror, mirror on the wall,
Do I really look so ________
Aged Bloated Cadaverous Disgusting
Elephantine Flamboyant Grotesque
Haphazard Intelligent Jittery Knobbly
Languid Menacing Nervous Owlish
Plump Queasy Rotund Scrawny
Toothy Ugly Voluptuous Wet
eXotic Yellow Zany?

Mirror, mirror on the wall,
I don't look like that at all!

The Minister's Cat

Did You Know?

When you say what something is like, you describe it by using ADJECTIVES.
ADJECTIVES answer the question, 'What kind of?' If a NOUN gives you a picture, ADJECTIVES help to colour it in, they make it more interesting. You can change a picture just by using a different ADJECTIVE.
'A *rosy* apple' is different from 'a *wormy* apple'. 'A *fat, chirpy* budgie' is different from 'a *pale, moulting* budgie'.

Word Game

Write a list of ADJECTIVES, one for each letter of the alphabet, to describe school, a season of the year, a trip to the sea or anything else you like. You can cheat with 'X' and use 'ex'.

The Minister's Cat is an Amiable cat and his name is Archie.
The Minister's Cat is a Beautiful cat and her name is Bubbles.
The Minister's Cat is a Cuddly cat and his name is Cupid.
The Minister's Cat is a Dashing cat and his name is Darcy.
The Minister's Cat is an Elegant cat and her name is Eglantine.
The Minister's Cat is a Fancy cat and his name is Ferdinand Forsyth-Fortescue.
The Minister's Cat is a Gorgeous cat and his name is George.
The Minister's Cat is a Hefty cat and his name is Hubert.
The Minister's Cat is an Independent cat and his name is It.

The Minister's Cat is a Jumping cat and his name is Jodhpurs.
The Minister's Cat is a Knitted cat and her name is Knickers.
The Minister's Cat is a Loony cat and his name is Lupin.
The Minister's Cat is a Miserable cat and his name is Mooch.
The Minister's Cat is a Noisy cat and his name is Mr Nobody.
The Minister's Cat is an Operatic cat and his name is Othello.
The Minister's Cat is a Popular cat and her name is Pussy.
The Minister's Cat is a Questing cat and his name is Quixote.
The Minister's Cat is a Ragged cat and his name is Rascal.
The Minister's Cat is a Scruffy cat and his name is Shrimp.
The Minister's Cat is a Tattered cat and his name is Troubadour.
The Minister's Cat is a Unique cat and his name is Ubu.
The Minister's Cat is a Versatile cat and her name is Vaudeville.
The Minister's Cat is a Waltzing cat and his name is Whirligig.
The Minister's Cat is an eXplosive cat and his name is Exodus.
The Minister's Cat is a Yowling cat and his name is Yorick.
The Minister's Cat is a Zestful cat and his name is Zebedee.

Word Game

Play the Minister's Cat with your friends. Take it in turns to describe the cat, going through the alphabet.

You may also like to write your own alphabetical list like the one above.

Verbal Dodgems

Come on everybody, let's take a whirl,
Take your seats on the bumper cars.
Think you're brill?
Then try your skill,
Give yourself a thrill
On the bumper cars.
Got fast reactions?
Up to you to prove.
Dodge or bump!
It's the verbs that make 'em move.

A . . . Avoid it
B . . . Bump it
C . . . Chase it
D . . . Dodge it
Expel it
Fight back
Glide away
Hit it!
Inch away

BUMPER CARS

Jump out of the way
Kick it away
Lie in wait
Move forward
Nudge alongside
Overtake
Pass by
Quicken up
Ram!
Swerve
Tear away
U-turn
Venture forward
Wham!
X-cross over
Y – I yield
Zigzag away.

Verbal Play

Did You Know? VERBS are words that make your pictures move. VERBS help things to get from one place to another. They also help people to think, to dream, to do anything they want. VERBS are words that bring NOUNS to life. Choose any situation and watch it come to life as the VERBS show what is happening.

A Class Discussion

A *a*rgued, B *b*oasted, C *c*hanged his mind constantly. D *d*oubted everything, E *e*xamined the points, F *f*idgeted, G *g*rabbed the hair of the girl in front. H *h*eard it all but said nothing, I was *i*nspired to heights of idiocy, J *j*umped in all the time, K *k*icked Sidney under the table. L *l*ooked out of the window, M did not *m*ince her words, N *n*odded off to sleep. O was too *o*pinionated, P *p*ut his foot in it. Q *q*uestioned everything and everybody, R *r*ubbed everyone up the wrong way. S was *s*ent out of the room, T *t*ied her tongue in a twist, U was *u*ncommitted, V *v*oted to go home, W *was w*eary of the whole thing. X e*x*pected everyone to agree with him, Y *y*awned noisily and Z just went to *zzzzz*.

Putting it Bluntly

"I can't see the point," he said *bluntly*.
"You can't get more blunt than that," she said *sharply*.
"She's as thick as two short planks," he said *woodenly*.
"Watch out, or I'll blow my top!" she said *explosively*.
"You'll be the death of me," he said *gravely*.
"I'll set my dog on you," she said *pettily*.
"You haven't got one," he said *dogmatically*.

Did You Know? (they asked questioningly!)
A word which tells you *how* something is done is called an ADVERB. That means that it ADDS TO THE VERB. ('Bluntly' tells you how it was said.)

Word Game

Try making up sentences like the ones above. Make sure your sentence leads up to your ADVERB. Try to be funny, we suggest *jokingly*.

Word Game

The ADVERB GAME is for a group to play.
One person leaves the room and everyone else agrees on one adverb (it might be 'grumpily'). On returning to the room, the person asks each member of the group to act a simple task 'in the manner of the adverb'. The aim is for that person to guess the adverb.

Dig the garden.
Peg out the clothes.
Build a house.
Serve a meal.

The Exquisite Corpse

Did You Know? This game was invented and played by a group of artists who liked to experiment with ideas that were out of the ordinary.
Surprise and chance played a part in this game.

Word Game

THE EXQUISITE CORPSE is a game of chance, played like Consequences, where words come together at random to make funny and peculiar sentences. Sometimes the sentences also have a ring of truth about them. Whatever happens, they can make you see things in a different way. There are two ways you might play the game.

1 Consequences

Fold a piece of paper into five columns.
Write the headings at the top of each column.

	ADJECTIVE	NOUN	VERB	ADJECTIVE	NOUN
1					
2					
3					
4					
5					

* Write down five adjectives in the first column. Fold the paper so you cannot see what you have written.
* Write down five nouns in the second column. Fold back the paper.
* Write down five verbs. Fold back.
* Write down five more adjectives. Fold back.
* Write down five more nouns. Unfold the whole paper.

2 Lucky Dip

You can also have three boxes. Fill them with adjectives, nouns and verbs.

ADJECTIVE	NOUN	VERB	ADJECTIVE	NOUN
1 simple	bottle	remembered	grateful	runner bean
2 chaotic	ringworm	punched	ancient	sunbeam
3 hazy	saucepan	spun	bronzed	hedgerow
4 sunny	owl	floated	bristly	mouse
5 purple	satellite	circled	negative	frog

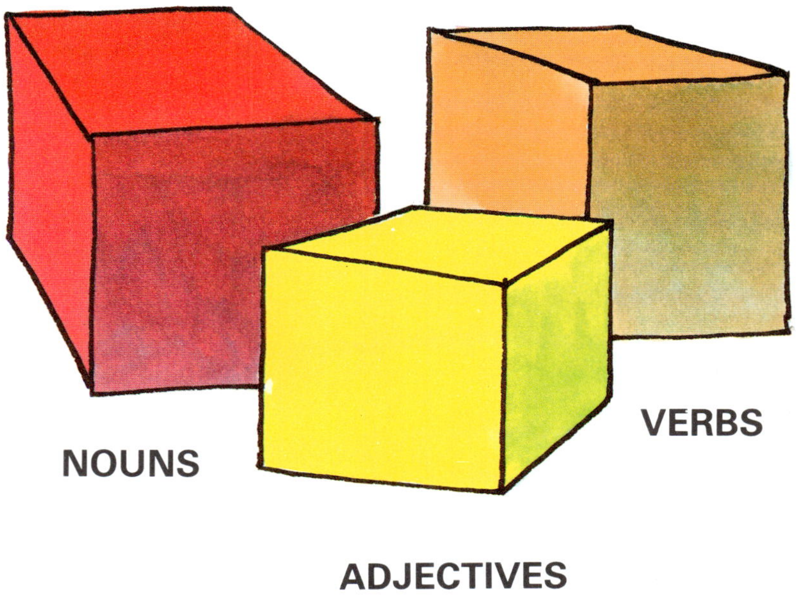

Now read out the sentences across each line, putting in words like ‘a’, ‘the’, ‘in’ and ‘over’, where you need them.

The simple bottle remembered *a* grateful runner bean.

A chaotic ringworm punched *an* ancient sunbeam.

A hazy saucepan spun *in a* bronzed hedgerow.

Then pull out words in the following order to make sentences:

Adjective, Noun, Verb, Adjective, Noun.

Telegrams

Word Game

TELEGRAMS is a game where you write a message, using the letters of a chosen word.

Each word of the message begins with the letters of your chosen word. We use 'WORD GAMES' for these telegrams. Why not try your own?

Names of people, countries and towns are often used.

HOLLAND – Hope Our Love Lasts And Never Dies!

Did You Know?

A MNEMONIC is a word that means a line or verse to help you remember something.

Richard Of York Gave Battle In Vain.

This helps you remember the order of the colours of the rainbow – *Red*, *Orange*, *Yellow*, *Green*, *Blue*, *Indigo*, *Violet*.

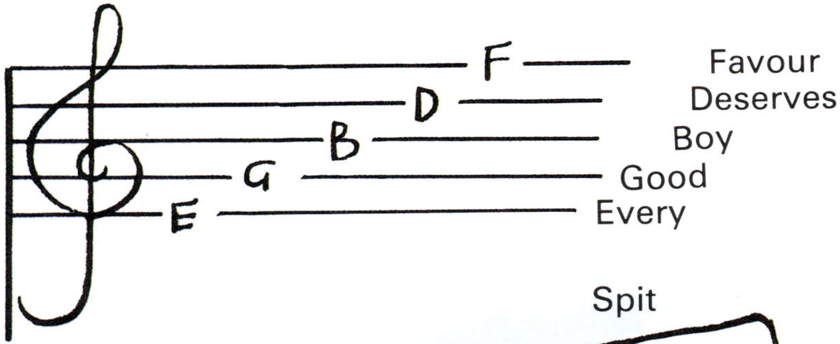

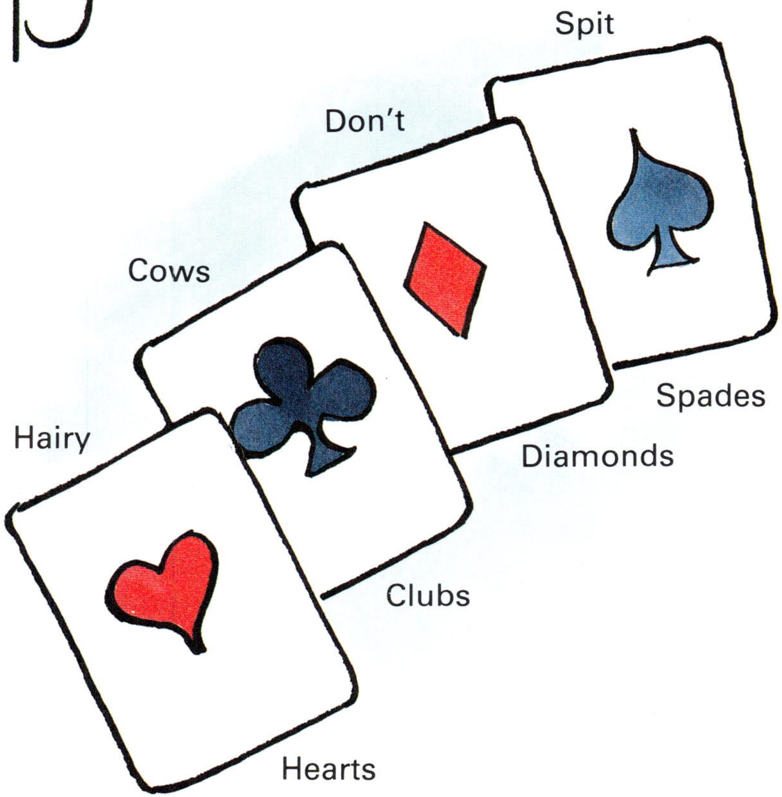

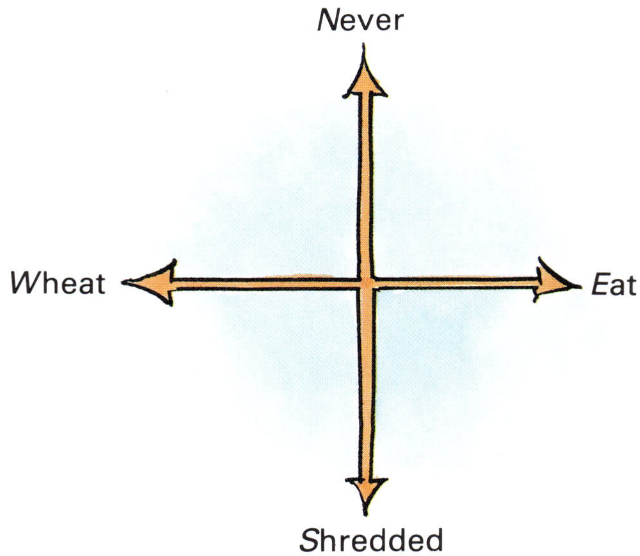

Word Game

You can make up your own mnemonics. You can even sing them to popular tunes.

What do you need to remember? The four seasons, the four elements, Kings and Queens of England?

Acrostics

W ords are all shapes and sizes,
O ften they are thin and streaky
R acing over the lines of a page,
D ashing ahead of the rest of the field,
G old medallists in banter and backchat.
A t other times they sit and ponder,
M ere spectators observing the sport.
E xtrovert words boast and bluster.
S uch is the stuff that dreams are made on.

Did You Know? An ACROSTIC is a word puzzle or poem in which the first (or last) letters of each line make a word or words.

Word Game

To write an ACROSTIC of your own, you could choose a word which will provide the subject of your poem. Write the word down the page and start each line with those letters.

P addington's imagination was to his own disadvantage,
A lways getting himself into trouble,
D aily entrusting himself into the hands of fate.
D oomed by his will to help.
I n Windsor Gardens things are never quiet.
N ose tingling at the thought of another adventure,
G rossly indulged in eating a sandwich,
T atty old hat upon his head,
O range marmalade shines on his snout.
N ever knows what will happen next.

Ben Owen

Spoonerisms

SPOONER SAID
A well-boiled icicle
A half-warmed fish
The Lord is a shoving leopard
He's a boiled sprat

INSTEAD OF
A well-oiled bicycle
A half-formed wish
The Lord is a loving shepherd
He's a spoiled brat

Did You Know? There was a man called the Reverend W. A. Spooner who used to mix his words up. He gave his name to SPOONERISMS like these where the first letters of words change places.

Word Game
Make up some SPOONERISMS of your own. They should make sense, like those above.

The Computer's First Christmas Card

jollymerry
hollyberry
jollyberry
merryholly
happyjolly
jollyjelly
jellybelly
bellymerry
hollyheppy
jollyMolly
marryJerry
merryHarry
hoppyBarry
heppyJarry
boppyheppy
berryjorry
jorryjelly
moppyjelly
Mollymerry
Jerryjolly
bellyboppy
jorryhoppy
hollymoppy
barrymerry
Jarryhappy
happyboppy
boppyjolly
jollymerry
merrymerry
merrymerry
merryChris
asamerryasa
Chrismerry
asMERRYCHR
YSANTHEMUM

Edwin Morgan

My Heart was in my Mouth

– you must be joking!

I have eyes in the back of my head.
I laughed my head off.
I was all fingers and thumbs.
He is looking daggers at me.
I was tongue-tied.
I'm laughing up my sleeve.

I SAY, I SAY–
Why couldn't the skeleton go to the dance?

Because he had no body to go with!

All dressed up like a dog's dinner.
Cat got your tongue?
You chickened out.
You're like a cat on hot bricks.

Word Game

How many expressions like these can you find?
You might draw pictures to go with them.

Foolish Questions

Where can a man buy a cap for his knee?
Or a key for the lock of his hair?
And can his eyes be called at school?
I would think – there are pupils there.
What jewels are found in the crown of his head,
And who walks on the bridge of his nose?
Can he use, in building the roof of his mouth,
The nails on the ends of his toes?
Can the crook of his elbow be sent to jail –
If it can, well, then what did it do?
And how does he sharpen his shoulder blades?
I'll be hanged if I know – do you?
Can he sit in the shade of the palm of his hand,
And beat time with the drum of his ear?
Can the calf of his leg eat the corn on his toe? –
There's somethin' pretty strange around here!

American Folk Rhyme
Adapted by *William Cole*

The Cheetah, my Dearest

The cheetah, my dearest, is known not to cheat;
the tiger possesses no tie;
the horse-fly, of course, was never a horse;
the lion will not tell a lie.

The turkey, though perky, was never a Turk;
nor the monkey ever a monk;
the mandrel, though like one, was never a man,
but some men are like him when drunk.

The springbok, dear thing, was not born in the Spring;
the walrus will not build a wall.
No badger is bad; no adder can add.
There is no truth in these things at all.

George Barker

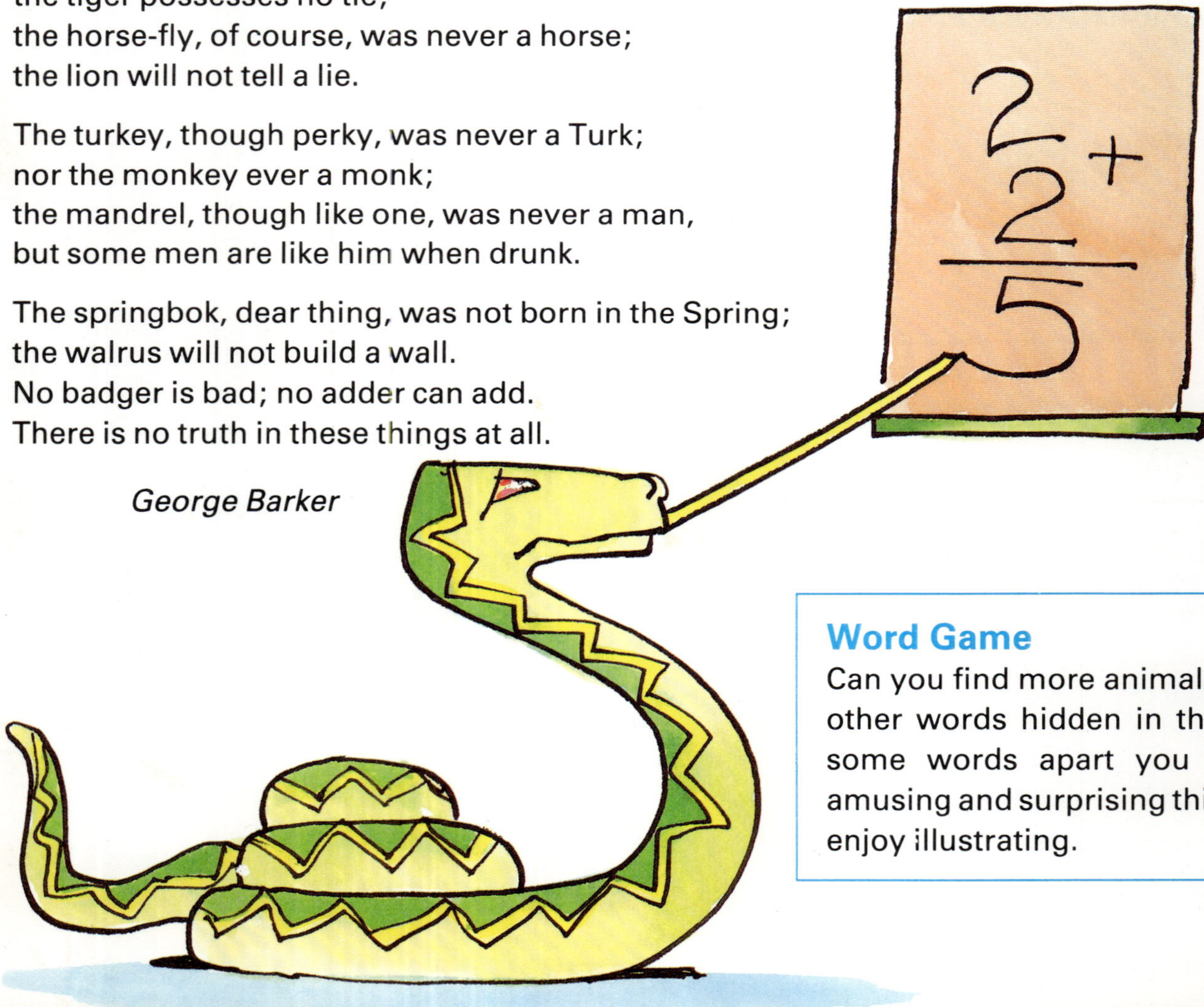

Cobra
Hedgehog
Jersey Cow
Gooseberry
Doldrums
Steeplechase

Word Game

Can you find more animals whose names have other words hidden in them? When you take some words apart you can discover some amusing and surprising things which you might enjoy illustrating.

Word Game

DAFT DEFINITIONS – try giving definitions for words like those here. Write them like riddles or jokes.
Ask other people to work out the answers.
doldrums – toy rhythm section.
lemonade – helpful citrus fruit (aid!)

Can you guess these characters from literature?

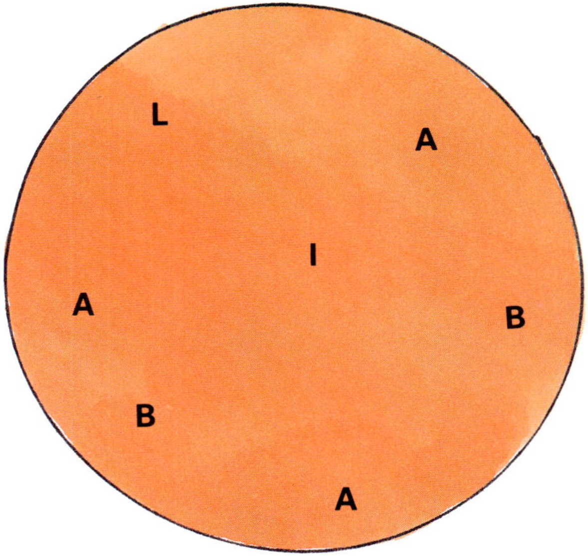

Arab sheepsong

Extra-wicked sailor

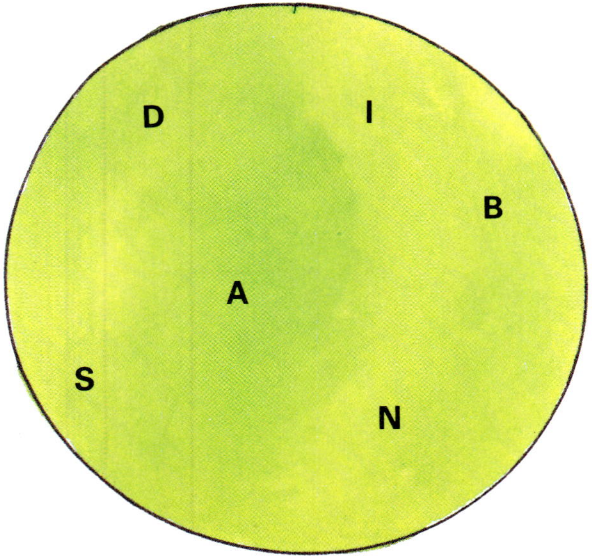

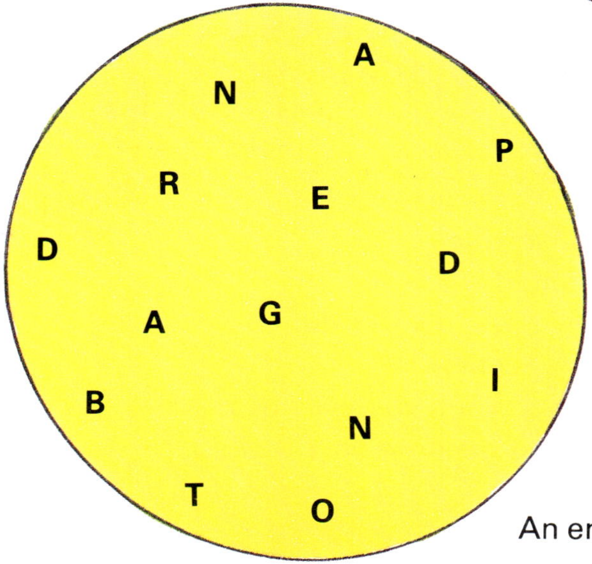

An empty railway station

Kennings

Four stiff standers
Four dilly danders
Two lookers
Two crookers
And a wig-wag.

Did You Know? The Vikings used KENNINGS in their poetry. KENNINGS are ways of describing something without using its proper name. KENNINGS usually describe what the thing is like or what it does.
A 'wig-wag' is a tail. 'Crookers' are horns.
A 'goggle-box' is a television set.
The American Indians called whisky 'fire-water' and a railway train 'the iron-horse'.
'See-saw' is a descriptive KENNING.
When you are up, you *see*, when you are down you *saw*! But this name has become the proper name now.

Word Game

Make up some KENNINGS for some of these: Earth, Rainbow, Sea, Fire, Winter, Books, Cars, Cat. Think of words that describe your subject and use those as your KENNINGS.

book – fact-finder, word-smithy
cat – milk-licker, mouse-catcher

Black Dot

a black dot
a jelly tot

a water-wriggler
a tail-jiggler

a cool kicker
a sitting slicker

a panting puffer
a fly-snuffer

a high hopper
a belly-flopper

a catalogue
to make me
frog.

Libby Houston

The Main-Deep

The long-rolling
Steady-pouring
Deep-troubled
Green-billow:

The wide-topped
Unbroken,
Green-glacid,
Slow-sliding

Cold-flushing,
-On-on-on-
Chill-rushing
Hush-hushing,

. . .Hush-hushing . . .

James Stephens

Anagrams

Juggling with letters.
How many ways can you juggle the letters of WORD GAMES to say something else?
You must use all the letters.

EGAD! WORMS!

GREW SO MAD

REG WAS MOD

MEGAWORDS

SWORD GAME

DAMES GROW

AGED WORMS

WARMED SOG

Have You Ever Noticed?

EVIL is an ANAGRAM of
LIVE
and VEIL
and VILE
and LEVI

TIME can become
MITE
or ITEM
or EMIT

SALT might be LAST

TEAM can be
MATE
or MEAT
or TAME

FIRE is RIFE

Word Game

Can you make an ANAGRAM of your name?

PETER PAN

T N E A E P P R

PAPER NET

New counting systems

While shepherds watched their flocks by night
Counting sheep one by one,
To save from getting bored they made
New counting rhymes for fun.

1	een	aina
2	teen	peina
3	tuther	par
4	futher	peddera
5	fip	pimp
6	sother	ithy
7	lother	mithy
8	porter	owera
9	dubber	lowera
10	dick	dig

Do You Know? Do you know any play-ground rhymes?

eeny meeny mackeracker
air I dominacker
chickericker om pom push.

Word Game

You can make up your own counting system with made-up words, or with words you find in the dictionary. Say it out loud to hear if it runs well and sounds good.
You might even take a theme, like food, or musical instruments.

onion	oboe
toffee	tuba
treacle	trumpet
fennel	flute
fig	fife
cinnamon	saxophone
sardine	vibraphone
endive	xylophone
noodle	sackbut
tart	gong

Counting in a foreign language can be fun too. Ask your friends if they can count in another language.

Ladles and Jellyspoons

Ladles and Jellyspoons:
I come before you
To stand behind you
And tell you something
I know nothing about.

Word Game

Ladles and Jellyspoons is, of course, another way of saying Ladies and Gentlemen. You can do the same thing with other pairs of words, like
Bubbles and Blisters for Brothers and Sisters,
Chuckles and Grunts for Uncles and Aunts,
Tease and Tickle for Cheese and Pickle.
Make sure your new names go together as a pair too.

Mean Song

Snickles and podes
Ribble and grodes:
That's what I wish you.

A nox in the groot,
A root in the stoot
And a gock in the forbeshaw, too.

Keep out of sight
For fear I might
Glom you a gravely snave.

Don't show your face
Around any place
Or you'll get one flack snack in the bave.

Eve Merriam

Word Game

One way of making up new words is to take two words from the dictionary and squash them together to make another word.

'Clot' and 'Stick-in-the-mud' could make Clud.
'Stupid' and 'Idiotic' could make Studiotic.
'Shouting' and 'Bickering' could make Shickering.

Stop shickering, you studiotic clud!

Try making up new words to describe the sea.
'Sparkling' and 'bright' become 'spright'.
'Waves' and 'shimmering' become 'wimmering'.

Sink Song

Scouring out the porridge pot,
  Round and round and round!

Out with all the scraith and scoopery,
Lift the eely, ooly droopery.
Chase the glubbery, slubbery gloopery
  Round and round and round!

Out with all the doleful dithery,
Ladle out the slimy slithery,
Hunt and catch the hithery thithery,
  Round and round and round!

Out with all the obbly gubbly,
On the stove it burns so bubbly,
Use the spoon and use it doubly,
  Round and round and round!

J. A. Lindon

Jabberwocky

'Twas brillig, and the slithy toves
Did gyre and gimble in the wabe;
All mimsy were the borogoves,
And the mome raths outgrabe.

"Beware the Jabberwock, my son!
The jaws that bite, the claws that catch!
Beware the Jubjub bird, and shun
The frumious Bandersnatch!"

He took his vorpal sword in hand:
Long time the manxome foe he sought –
So rested he by the Tumtum tree,
And stood awhile in thought.

And as in uffish thought he stood,
The Jabberwock, with eyes of flame,
Came whiffling through the tulgey wood,
And burbled as it came!

One, two! One, two! And through and through
The vorpal blade went snicker-snack!
He left it dead, and with its head
He went galumphing back.

"And hast thou slain the Jabberwock!
Come to my arms, my beamish boy!
O frabjous day! Callooh! Callay!"
He chortled in his joy.

'Twas brillig, and the slithy toves
Did gyre and gimble in the wabe;
All mimsy were the borogoves,
And the mome raths outgrabe.

From Through the Looking-Glass and What Alice Found There

"Would you kindly tell me the meaning of the poem called 'Jabberwocky'?"

"Let's hear it," said Humpty Dumpty. "I can explain all the poems that ever were invented – and a good many that haven't been invented just yet."

This sounded very hopeful, so Alice repeated the first verse:

"'Twas brillig, and the slithy toves
Did gyre and gimble in the wabe:
All mimsy were the borogoves,
And the mome raths outgrabe."

"That's enough to begin with," Humpty Dumpty interrupted: "there are plenty of hard words there. '*Brillig*' means four o'clock in the afternoon – the time when you begin *broiling* things for dinner."

"That'll do very well," said Alice: "and '*slithy*'?"

"Well, '*slithy*' means 'lithe and slimy.' 'Lithe' is the same as 'active'. You see it's like a portmanteau – there are two meanings packed up into one word."

"I see it now," Alice remarked thoughtfully: "and what are '*toves*'?"

"Well, '*toves*' are something like badgers – they're something like lizards – and they're something like corkscrews."

"They must be very curious creatures."

"They are that," said Humpty Dumpty: "also they make their nests under sun-dials – also they live on cheese."

"And what's to '*gyre*' and to '*gimble*'?"

"To '*gyre*' is to go round and round like a gyroscope. To '*gimble*' is to make holes like a gimlet."

"And '*the wabe*' is the grass-plot round a sun-dial, I suppose?" said Alice, surprised at her own ingenuity.

"Of course it is. It's called '*wabe*', you know, because it goes a long way before it, and a long way behind it –"

"And a long way beyond it on each side," Alice added.

"Exactly so. Well then, '*mimsy*' is 'flimsy and miserable' (there's another portmanteau for you). And a '*borogove*' is a thin shabby-looking bird with its feathers sticking out all round – something like a live mop."

'And then '*mome raths*'?" said Alice. "If I'm not giving you too much trouble."

"Well, a '*rath*' is a sort of green pig: but '*mome*' I'm not certain about. I think it's short for 'from home' – meaning that they'd lost their way, you know."

"And what does '*outgrabe*' mean?"

"Well, '*outgribing*' is something between bellowing and whistling, with a kind of sneeze in the middle: however, you'll hear it done, maybe – down in the wood yonder – and when you've once heard it you'll be *quite* content."

Lewis Carroll

A CIRCUS OF WORDS

Words you can juggle – throw up from one hand to another.

hurdygurdy niminypiminy

helterskelter teetertotter

topsyturvy dillydally

Words that clown about and play the fool.

mollycoddle nincompoop collywobbles

ribald sausages taradiddle

Words that snarl back at you and must be tamed with the tongue.

whippersnapper

cacophony

dogmatic

intergalactic

Words that somersault like

bric -a- brac

mar zi pan

Word Game

Collect words that you like the sound of. Look in a dictionary. Find words that sound like circus acts.

Words that walk the tightrope like

Words that perform on the flying trapeze like

Word Game

Collect words whose *sounds* show how you feel when you are angry, sad, happy and in other moods.

Word Game

FLOWER INSULTS – ever wanted a good name to call somebody, a name that won't get you into trouble? Try looking in a wild flower book and collecting the names you find there. Have an interesting sounding argument with someone and use them!

You're nothing but a common scurvy-grass and a bulbous buttercup too!
Oh, just listen to her, such a scarlet pimpernel, a stinging nettle.
You pignut!
Bogbean!
Spotted medick!
Dandelion!
I hate you, you great big hairy bitter-cress!
Language, language, you stinking chamomile. And as for her, she's little better than a reflexed stonecrop.
Just a minute, you overgrown pedunculate oak!
Only a squill could use language like that – a squill and a welted thistle!

Hugger Mugger

I'd sooner be
Jumped and thumped and dumped,
I'd sooner be
Slugged and mugged . . . than *hugged* . . .
And clobbered with a slobbering
Kiss by my Auntie Jean:

You know what I mean?

Whenever she comes to stay,
You know you're bound
To get one.
A quick short peck would be O.K.
But this is a
Whacking great
Smacking great
Wet one!
All whoosh and spit
And crunch and squeeze
And '*Dear* little boy!'
And 'Auntie's missed you!'
And 'Come to Auntie, she
Hasn't *kissed* you!'
Please don't do it, Auntie,
PLEASE!

Or if you've absolutely
Got to,

And nothing on *earth* can
persuade you
Not to,

The trick
Is to make it
Quick,

You know what I mean?

For as things are,
I really would far,

Far sooner be
Jumped and thumped and dumped,

I'd sooner be
Slugged and mugged . . .
than *hugged*

And clobbered with a slobbering
Kiss by my Auntie

Jean!

Kit Wright

Which Witch?

Whether the weather be fine
Or whether the weather be not,
Whether the weather be cold
Or whether the weather be hot,
We'll weather the weather,
Whatever the weather,
Whether we like it or not.

Did You Know? Words that sound the same but are spelt differently are called HOMOPHONES.

hymn and him   which and witch
whether and weather   queue, cue and Kew

Word Game
How many HOMOPHONES can you collect?
You might find the dictionary helpful.

Did You Know? PALINDROMES are words or sentences that read the same backwards as forwards.
LEVEL is a PALINDROME.
MADAM is one too.

What did the first man say to the first woman?

Madam, I'm Adam.

Probably the cleverest PALINDROME of all is:
A MAN, A PLAN, A CANAL – PANAMA.

Word Game
See how many PALINDROMIC words or phrases you can find.
mum   dad   bob   did

I SAY, I SAY – What do you get if you cross a witch with an ice-cube?

A cold spell!

Did You Know? Words which are spelt the same but mean different things are called HOMONYMS.

SPELL can mean – what witches chant,
or – in what order you write the letters of a word,
or – a short stretch of time.

WELL can mean – not ill,
or – a hole in the ground for drawing water.

Doctor Bell fell down a well
And broke his collar bone,
Doctors should attend the sick
And leave the well alone.

Word Game

How many HOMONYMS can you find?
You could keep a book for all your collections of words.

What's the Difference?

How many ways can you say the same thing?

The End of the Road

In these boots and with this staff
Two hundred leaguers and a half
Walked I, went I, paced I, tripped I,
Marched I, held I, skelped I, slipped I,
Pushed I, panted, swung and dashed I;
Picked I, forded, swam and splashed I,
Strolled I, climbed I, crawled and scrambled,
Dropped and dipped I, ranged and rambled;
Plodded I, hobbled I, trudged and tramped I,
And in lonely spinnies camped I,
Lingered, loitered, limped and crept I,
Clambered, halted, stepped and leapt I,
Slowly sauntered, roundly strode I,
And . . .
Let me not conceal it . . . rode I.

Hilaire Belloc

Word Game

How many words can you find that mean 'to move'?

One class of children found 303!

TO MOVE

crawl
teeter
scuttle
hop
fly
meander
sidle
walk
budge

Did You Know? Words which mean nearly the same thing are called SYNONYMS.

ship – vessel – boat – barque – barge

soft – tender – gentle – mild – velvety

Word Game

You can also collect SYNONYMS for the verb 'to speak'. You will find that some of them rhyme. Play a game with a friend as if you were playing a game of tennis. Take it in turns to serve (speak) a word and your friend has to say a SYNONYM that rhymes. He then serves a word to you. If he cannot find a rhyme you win a point. The first one to reach 10 is the winner.

The Kangaroo's Coff

A Poem for Children Ill in Bed, Indicating to Them
the Oddities of our English Orthography

The eminent Professor Hoff
Kept, as a pet, a Kangaroo
Who, one March day, started a coff
That very soon turned into floo.

Before the flu carried him off
To hospital (still with his coff),
A messenger came panting through
The door, and saw the Kangarough.

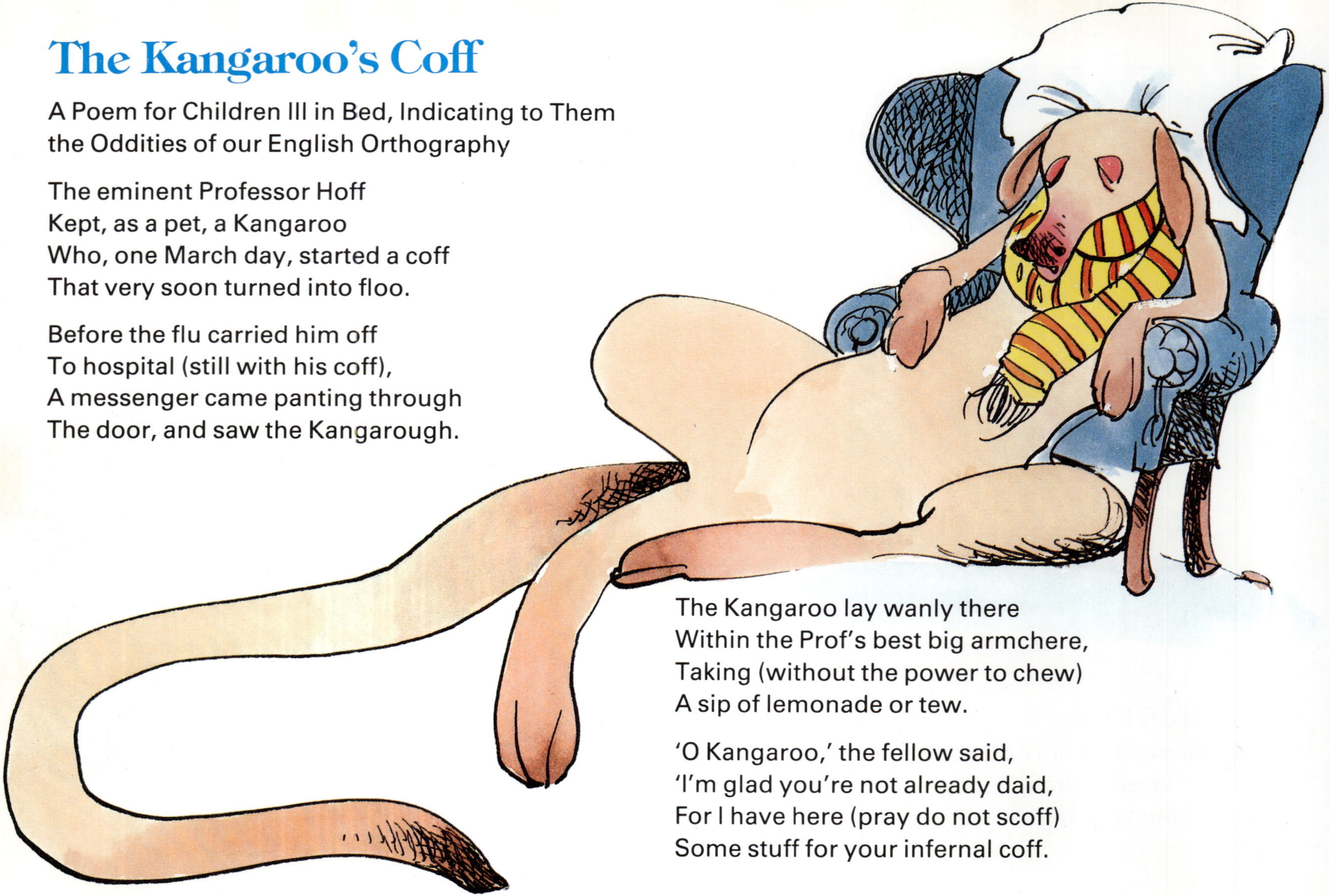

The Kangaroo lay wanly there
Within the Prof's best big armchere,
Taking (without the power to chew)
A sip of lemonade or tew.

'O Kangaroo,' the fellow said,
'I'm glad you're not already daid,
For I have here (pray do not scoff)
Some stuff for your infernal coff.

'If you will take these powdered fleas,
And just a tiny lemon squeas
Mixed with a little plain tapwater,
They'll cure you. Or at least they ater.'

Prof Hoff then fixed the medicine,
Putting the fleas and lemon ine
A glass of water, which he brought
The Kangaroo as he'd been tought.

The Kangaroo drank down the draught,
Shivered and scowled – then oddly laught
And vaulted out of the armchair
Before the Prof's astonished stair –

Out of the window, in the air
Up to the highest treetop whair
He sat upon the topmost bough
And chortled down, 'Look at me nough!'

The messenger would not receive
Reward for this, but answered, 'Weive
Done our best, and that's reward
Enough, my very learned lard'

(By which he meant Professor Hoff).
As for the Kangaroo, he blew
A kiss down as the man rode off,
A cured and happy Kangarew –

As you may be, when you have read
This tale I wrote lying in bead.

Anthony Thwaite

Whizz! Bang! Plonk!

Oink!
Quack!
Woof!
Gobble! Gobble!
Baa!
Miaow!
Moo!
Hiss!
Cuckoo!
Squawk!

Did You Know? When you use words which sound like the noise things make you are using ONOMATOPOEIA (*on-o-mat-o-pee-a*).
There are many 'sound' words for speaking – grunt, whisper, screech, murmur, giggle, guffaw.
Say them out loud and hear the sounds.

Whisper, Whisper

Whisper whisper
whisper whisper
goes my sister
down the phone

Whisper whisper
go the beech leaves
breathing in the
wind alone

Whisper whisper
whisper whisper
slips the river
on the stone

Whisper whisper
go my parents
when they whisper
on their own

I don't mind the
whisper whisper
whisper whisper
it's a tune

Sometimes though
I wish the whisper
whisperings would
shut up soon.

Kit Wright

Word Game

Make collections of ONOMATOPOEIC words.
If they are words that make voice sounds you can draw a large mouth and write them coming out of it. Try the sounds of movement (hobble, squelch, tramp, tiptoe) and group them round a picture of feet.
You can try describing something like the sea or a storm, using ONOMATOPOEIC words.

Sea Shell

Lift to your ear
The gleaming wave-washed shell,
Its song may tell
Strange ocean fantasies
Of silver pearls,
Glimpsed through the restless surge,
Of slender sinuous weeds
That golden patterns weave
By banks of bright anemones;
Of fishes, rainbow finned;
Of secret twilight caves
Where tides, their fury tamed,
Go stealing tip-toe in.

Enid Madoc-Jones

The Loch Ness Monster's Song

Sssnnnwhuffffll?
Hnwhuffl hhnnwfl hnfl hfl?
Gdroblboblhobngbl gbl gl gg g g g glbgl.
Drublhaflablhaflubhafgabhaflhafl fl fl –
bm grawwww grf grawf awfgm graw gm.
Hovoplodok-doplodovok-plovodokot-
doplodokosh?
Splgraw fok fok splgrafhatchgabrlgabrl fok splfok!
Zgra kra gka fok!
Grof grawff gahf?
Gombl mbl bl-
blm plm,
blm plm,
blm plm,
blp.

Edwin Morgan

Word Game

Make up some ONOMATOPOEIC words of your own to describe the sounds made when doing something like walking through piles of leaves, at a firework display, or swimming underwater.

Here, There and Everywhere

Say 'Aaagh!'

No fun being the dentist.
Not much fun as a job.
Spending all of your days in gazing
Right into everyone's gob.

No fun seeing the dentist.
Not much fun at all:
Staring straight up his hairy nostrils –
Drives you up the wall.

Kit Wright

Did You Know? Words telling you where something is, are called PREPOSITIONS:
over, under, round, inside, outside, below, above.

PREPOSITIONS make you look at something from different positions.

Word Game

Make a list of PREPOSITIONS. Using these, write about something (My Head, The Window, The Sea, or anything else you like), looking at it from different positions. Start each line with a new PREPOSITION.

Behind my head lives sadness without life,
Inside my head swims a paradise world,
Around my head lie clouds dizzy from the wind.
Far from my head are shadows melting quickly,
Beside my head stands another head
Reflecting.

Catriona Ferguson

Thirteen Ways of Looking at a Teddy Bear

How many ways are there of looking at something? There are as many as you can find.
You just need to look and use your imagination to see things from any number of different angles.

Word Game

There are two ways of playing this game.

1 Choose a subject to write about and write one verse at a time. Each verse will be a different way of looking at your subject. After each verse, rest for a moment and decide which angle you want next. The title of your poem will be '(your number) Ways of Looking at –'.
Write as many ways as you want, but try to write *at least* six.

Did You Know? There is a famous poem by Wallace Stevens called 'Thirteen Ways of Looking at a Blackbird', and another poem, that plays with this idea, by Peter Redgrove, called 'Thirteen Ways of Looking at a Blackboard'.
The poem 'Thirteen Ways of Looking at a Teddy Bear' was written by a group of children.

Word Game

2 Another way to play this game is for each member of a group to write one verse on the same subject. Collect all the verses together and decide amongst yourselves in which order to place them. The result will be a long poem to which everyone has contributed.

1 A blank sheet of brown
With two orange marbles
And some black lines.

2 A dark glove-puppet
For my mind's fingers.

3 It's a marble-eyed
Mathematician
In concentration.

4 Wandering around
His eyes just fix on you
As if you are the only
Thing that can comfort him.

5 Someone to tell your problems to.
Someone to sleep with.

6 A thing you tear to bits,
Swear at
And bury your tears in.

7 Something that gets
Pulled downstairs
By its ears.

8 Something to beat the hell out of
When you're cross,
A lump of fur for punching.

9 A way to tell a teddy
Is the icy, springy, itchy fur
To comfort and drain your tears away.

10 More important than a single toy.

11 Teddy dreams of going into the world
and becoming famous.
Of going into partnership with Tarzan,
Being a little saint among children.

12 A teddy's wish –
To shout back!

13 The world has changed,
Inflation and unemployment rise
But teddy's still got a job.

Horse

The horse at the shore
Casks of red apples, skull, a barrel of rum

The horse in the field
Plough, ploughman, gulls, a furrow, a cornstalk

The horse in the peat-bog
Twelve baskets of dark fire

The horse at the pier
Letters, bread, paraffin, one passenger, papers

The horse at the show
Ribbons, raffia, high bright hooves

The horse in the meadow
A stallion, a red wind, between the hills

The horse at the burn
Quenching a long flame in the throat

George Mackay Brown

Alternative Endings to an Unwritten Ballad

I stole through the dungeons, while everyone slept,
Till I came to the cage where the Monster was kept.
There, locked in the arms of a Giant Baboon,
Rigid and smiling, lay . . . MRS RAVOON!

I climbed the clock tower in the first morning sun
And 'twas midday at least 'ere my journey was done;
But the clock never sounded the last stroke of noon,
For there, from the clapper, swung MRS RAVOON!

I hauled in the line, and I took my first look
At the half-eaten horror that hung from the hook.
I had dragged from the depths of the limpid lagoon
The luminous body of MRS RAVOON.

I fled in the storm, the lightning and thunder,
And there, as a flash split the darkness asunder,
Chewing a rat's-tail and mumbling a rune,
Mad in the moat squatted MRS RAVOON!

I stood by the waters so green and so thick,
And I stirred at the scum with my old, withered stick;
When there rose through the ooze, like a monstrous
. . . balloon,
The bloated cadaver of MRS RAVOON.

Facing the fens, I looked back from the shore
Where all had been empty a moment before;
And there by the light of the Lincolnshire moon,
Immense on the marshes, stood . . . MRS RAVOON!

Paul Dehn

This poem is playing with the idea of having a number of different endings to a story (though the story has not been written). It is another way of looking at something from different angles. Whichever way you look at it Mrs Ravoon comes to a rather sticky end!

Word Game

Write some possible endings to a story in which the main character, Septimus Lee, first mate on the *Iron Lady*, is about to abandon the ship which has run aground on the rocks. Or you can invent your own character and situation.

Battle Lines

What I hate about spiders
Is their great big black hairy legs.

What I like about spiders
Is the way they spin such beautiful silky webs.

What I hate about spiders
Is the way they hide in corners
And creep up on you
When you least expect it.

What I like about spiders
Is the way they make some people scream
When you put them down their backs.

What I hate about spiders
Is when you're in the bath
And turn on the tap –
They come tumbling out on top of you.

What I like about spiders
Is the way they never give up.
They keep coming up the plughole
Even when you've washed them down.

Word Game

You need two teams for BATTLE LINES. One team is the LIKES and the other is the HATES. Choose a subject about which you can feel strongly (spiders, liver, mirrors, for example) and each person writes a sentence about the subject, either a LIKE or a HATE, depending on which team you are in. Check with the others in your team that you all have something different to say. Then let battle commence. With the teams facing each other, take it in turns to SHOUT out your sentences. Put as much feeling into your words as possible. You might like to write them down afterwards.

Horrible Things

'What's the horriblest thing you've seen?'
Said Nell to Jean.

'Some grey-coloured, trodden-on plasticine;
On a plate, a left-over cold baked bean;
A cloak-room ticket numbered thirteen;
A slice of meat without any lean;
The smile of a spiteful fairy-tale queen;
A thing in the sea like a brown submarine;
A cheese fur-coated in brilliant green,
A bluebottle perched on a piece of sardine.
What's the horriblest thing you've seen?'
Said Jean to Nell.

'Your face, as you tell
Of all the horriblest things you've seen!'

Roy Fuller

The Spider in the Bath

I have fought a grizzly bear,
Tracked a cobra to its lair,
Killed a crocodile who dared to cross my path;
But the thing I really dread
When I've just got out of bed
Is to find that there's a spider in the bath.

I've no fear of wasps or bees,
Mosquitos only tease,
I rather like a cricket on the hearth;
But my blood runs cold to meet
In pyjamas and bare feet
With a great big hairy spider in the bath.

I have faced a charging bull in Barcelona,
I have dragged a mountain lioness from her cub,
I've restored a mad gorilla to its owner
But I don't dare to face that Tub . . .

What a frightful-looking beast –
Half an inch across at least –
It would frighten even Superman or Garth.
There's contempt it can't disguise
In the little beady eyes
Of the spider sitting glowering in the bath.

It ignores my every lunge
With the back-brush and the sponge;
I have bombed it with 'A Present from Penarth';
But it doesn't mind at all –
It just rolls into a ball
And simply goes on squatting in the bath . . .

For hours we have been locked in endless struggle;
I have lured it to the deep end, by the drain;
At last I think I've washed it down the plug-'ole
But here it comes a-crawling up the chain!

Now it's time for me to shave
Though my nerves will not behave,
And there's bound to be a fearful aftermath;
So before I cut my throat
I shall leave this final note:
DRIVEN TO IT – BY THE SPIDER IN THE BATH!

Michael Flanders and *Donald Swann*

Lies

When we are bored
My friend and I
Tell
Lies.

It's a competition: the prize
Is won by the one
Whose lies
Are the bigger size.

We really do:
That's true.
But there isn't a prize:
That's lies.

Kit Wright

My Dad, Your Dad

My dad's fatter than your dad,
Yes, my dad's fatter than yours:
If he eats any more he won't fit in the house,
He'll have to live out of doors.

Yes, but my dad's balder than your dad,
My dad's balder, O.K.,
He's only got two hairs left on his head
And both are turning grey.

Ah, but my dad's thicker than your dad,
My dad's thicker, all right.
He has to look at his watch to see
If it's noon or the middle of the night.

Yes, but my dad's more boring than your dad.
If he ever starts counting sheep
When he can't get to sleep at night, he finds
It's the sheep that go to sleep.

But my dad doesn't mind your dad.
Mine quite likes yours too.
I suppose they don't always think much of US!
That's true, I suppose, that's true.

Kit Wright

Tall Stories

A farmer, tired of dry farming in desert country, decided to move house to a place of eternal rain. When he was asked why, he said, 'I'm tired of sweating dust, that's why. Out here the only rains are dust storms. Buzzards have to wear goggles and fly backwards to keep from choking to death, and grasshoppers carry haversacks to keep from starving. The only fish to be caught in dry lakes are dried herring, and my mouth is always so dry that I have to whistle to my dog by ringing a bell.'

A traveller from a wet region where the rain was almost continuous decided to move house. He explained, 'This place is too wet for me. The only time the sun ever shines is when it rains. Even the pores of my skin are sprouting watercress. I could stand it when water-bugs took the place of flies, and when the chickens grew webbed feet and their eggs hatched out turtles; I just laughed at the bull-frogs croaking on the head of my bed and when my wife got water on the knee. But when I started catching cat-fish in the sitting room mouse-trap I reckoned it was time to move.'

Anonymous American

Mean! He was so mean he wouldn't even let his dog drink from a mirage.

I'm that unlucky that if it rained soup, everybody would have a spoon and I'd be left with a fork.

'It was so cold where we were in Greece that the candle-light froze and we couldn't blow it out.'

'That's nothing. Where we were, the words came out of our mouths in pieces of ice, and we had to fry them to see what we were talking about.'

Traditional

Tall Stories

You're so thin you have to run around in the shower to get wet.

You're so incredibly thin that if you stood sideways and put out your tongue you'd look like a zip-fastener.

Word Game

To play TALL STORIES you need two teams. Imagine that something has happened (you do not need to know what). One team found it hilariously funny and the other team found it dreadfully awful. Each member of the team writes a sentence to say how funny, or how awful, the experience was. Then the teams line up opposite each other and take it in turns to say the sentences. It is like a competition to see who can invent the most unlikely sentence.

It was so funny I laughed my head off and had to ask someone to stick it back on for me.

It was so awful I wished the ground had swallowed me up and not even spat out the bones.

It was so funny even the birds were laughing so hard they fell out of the trees.

It was so awful that Anne Boleyn rejoiced since she'd only had her head cut off.

It was so funny that I laughed for a whole year and got into the Guinness Book of Records.

It was so awful I cried so much that they had to draw a new ocean on all the world maps.

Gift-Bringers

Extract from *The Sleeping Beauty*

All the Fairies began to give their gifts to the Princess. The youngest gave her for a gift that she should be the most beautiful person in the world; the next, that she should have the wit of an angel; the third, that she should have admirable grace in every thing she did; the fourth, that she should dance perfectly well; the fifth, that she should sing like a nightingale; and the sixth, that she should play upon all kinds of musick to the utmost perfection.

The old Fairy's turn coming next, with a head shaking more with spite than old age, she said that the Princess should have her hand pierced with a spindle and die of the wound. This terrible gift made the whole company tremble, and everybody fell a-crying.

Charles Perrault

Did You Know? The American Indians often used to give a new-born child a special name taken from the natural world, a name which they felt suited the child. They would sing lullabies whose words conjured up the way they would like the child to be.

From *The Song of Hiawatha*

With him dwelt his dark-eyed daughter,
Wayward as the Minnehaha,
With her moods of shade and sunshine,
Eyes that smiled and frowned alternate,
Feet as rapid as the river,
Tresses flowing like the water,
And as musical a laughter;
And he named her from the river,
From the waterfall he named her,
Minnehaha, Laughing Water.

Henry Wadsworth Longfellow

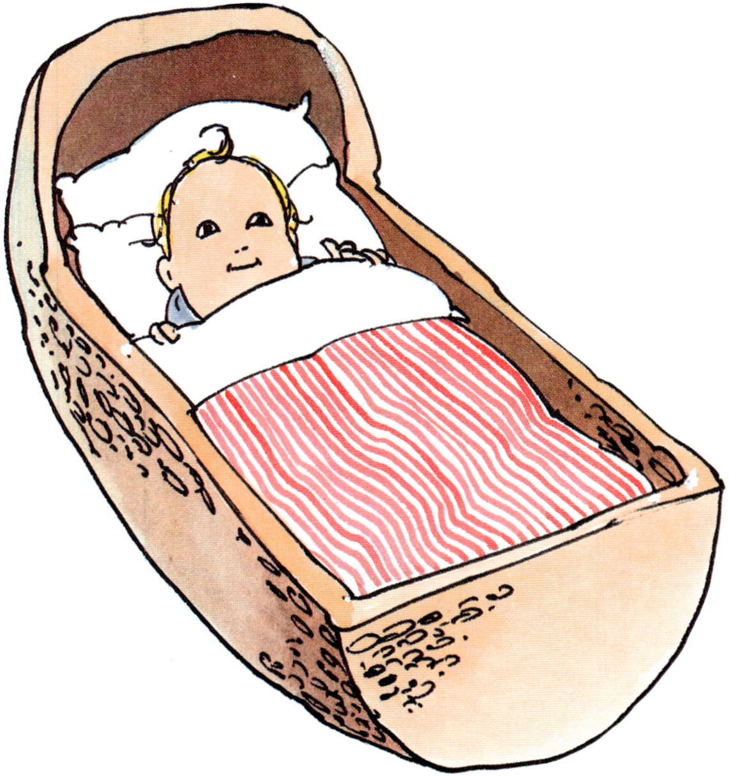

Lullaby for a New-Born Child

I give you a love of beechwoods in Spring,
And days spent walking over the moor,
I give you times when you will be alone
And eyes that know smiles and tears.
You will be loved by many friends
But some will be true and others false.
Do not stay too long in dreams,
The strength to move mountains easily dies.
I give you the busy sounds of Summer,
Learn from them and understand.
I give you, too, the stillness of Winter,
Let thoughts stay buried till they're ready to grow.

W. J. Bonso

Word Game

Write a lullaby for the naming of a child, in which you give gifts to help the child through life. These will be the kind of gifts you cannot normally give, like happiness, a sense of humour, the song of the skylark, the sunset over a calm sea.

Word Game

You could also write your last will and testament where you bequeath things to people. What you leave people in your will is not always something they are pleased to have. The thick fog of a November night, or the sharp nip of frost in January.

Last Wish

To you I grant a heart
For it is you who truly needs one.
I leave to you understanding
For though you seem to know it all
You are totally devoid of knowledge.
I take away from you the power to worship
For you seem not to want it.
I give you humility,
Practise having it in your possession.

Hedy-anne Goodman

We three kings of Orient are,
Bearing gifts we traverse afar,
Field and fountain, moor and mountain,
Following yonder star.

Chorus Oh, Star of Wonder, Star of Night,
Star with royal beauty bright,
Westward leading, still proceeding,
Guide us to thy perfect light.

Born a king on Bethlehem's plain,
Gold I bring to crown him again,
King for ever, ceasing never
Over us all to reign.

Frankincense to offer have I,
Incense owns a Deity nigh,
Prayer and praising, all men raising,
Follow him, God on high.

Myrrh is mine, its bitter perfume
Breathes a life of gathering gloom,
Sorrowing, sighing, bleeding, dying,
Sealed in the stone-cold tomb.

Glorious, now, behold him arise,
King, and God, and sacrifice,
Heaven sings 'Allelujah,'
'Allelujah,' the earth replies.

J. H. Hopkins

Glossary of Terms

Noun – a word that tells you the name of something,
e.g. London, Tracey, chair, dream.

Adjective – a word that tells you what something is like,
e.g. happy, red, nosy.

Verb – a word that tells you what something is doing,
e.g. walk, drown, think, slurp.

Adverb – a word that tells you *how* something is done,
e.g. revoltingly, swiftly, badly, well.

Preposition – a word that tells you where something is in relation to something else,
e.g. in, beside, around, between.

Acrostic – usually a poem where the first letters of each line spell a word.

Anagram – a mixing-up of the letters of a word in order to make another word.

Spoonerism – the swapping over of first letters of words to make a new phrase,
e.g. hoots from the ship
shoots from the hip.

Kennings – ways of describing things by what they are like and not by their proper names. They often combine two nouns,
e.g. wigwag for tail, fire-water for whisky.

Homophones – words that sound the same but are spelt differently,
e.g. knight and night, tail and tale, cue, Kew and queue.

Homonyms – words that are spelt and sound the same but can have different meanings,
e.g. spell, sentence, well.

Palindrome – a word, or phrase, that spells the same backwards as forwards,
e.g. level, rotor, Madam I'm Adam.

Synonyms – different words that have a similar meaning,
e.g. happy, joyful, cheerful;
sad, miserable, gloomy, blue.

Onomatopoeia – words, or phrases, whose sounds remind you of what they mean,
e.g. chatter, quack, squelch.

Index of Poems (Titles and First Lines)

Index of Poets

Acknowledgments

The authors and publisher would like to thank the following for permission to include copyright materials in this book:

Faber and Faber Ltd for 'The Cheetah, my Dearest' from *Runes and Rhymes and Tunes and Chimes* by George Barker; A D Peters and Co. Ltd for 'The End of the Road' by Hilaire Belloc from his *Sonnets and Verse* published by Gerald Duckworth and Co. Ltd; The Hogarth Press for 'The Horse at the Shore' by George Mackay Brown from his *Portrait of Orkney*; William Cole for his poem 'Foolish Questions', © William Cole; Catriona Ferguson for her poem 'Behind my Head'; The Estate of Michael Flanders and Lister Welch Ltd for 'The Spider in the Bath' by Michael Flanders and Donald Swann, © The Estate of Michael Flanders; André Deutsch Ltd for 'Horrible Things' by Roy Fuller from his *Seen Grandpa Lately*; Hedy-anne Goodman for her poem 'Last Wish'; Libby Houston for her poem 'Black Dot', originally commissioned and published by BBC Radio 4 Schools series *Stories and Rhymes*; Hazel J Lindon for 'Sink Song' by J A Lindon; Carcanet Press Ltd for 'The Computer's First Christmas Card' and 'The Loch Ness Monster's Song' by Edwin Morgan from his *Poems of Thirty Years*, © Edwin Morgan and published by Carcanet Press Ltd, Manchester, 1982; Ben Owen for his poem 'Paddington'; The Society of Authors on behalf of the copyright owner Mrs Iris Wise for 'The Main-Deep' by James Stephens; Anthony Thwaite for his poem 'The Kangaroo's Coff' from *Allsorts of Poems*; Penguin Books Ltd for 'Say "Aaagh!"' and 'Hugger Mugger' by Kit Wright, © Kit Wright 1981, from his *Hot Dog and Other Poems*; William Collins Sons and Co. Ltd for 'Lies', 'Whisper, Whisper' and 'My Dad, Your Dad' by Kit Wright from his *Rabbiting On*; Eve Merriam for her poem 'Mean Song' from *There is no Rhyme for Silver* by Eve Merriam, published by Atheneum Publishers, New York, copyright © 1962 by Eve Merriam, reprinted by permission of the author.

In certain cases it has not proved possible to contact copyright holders, but full acknowledgment will be made in later printings of any rights not mentioned here if the publisher is advised in writing of the omission.